I WANNA BE THE KINDA FATHER MY MOTHER WAS

OMANII
ABDULLAH

New Readers Press

Dedication

To my wife, Najla, who has been very
supportive of my writing.

To my mother, Addie Grace Ford,
the lifeline of our family.

To my sister, Roslyn Diane Grace, who
has shown me through her example that
you can do anything you want to if you
put your mind to it.

Copyright © 1993
 New Readers Press
U.S. Publishing Division of Laubach Literacy International
Box 131, Syracuse, New York 13210-0131

10   9   8   7   6   5   4

Library of Congress Cataloging-in-Publication Data

Abdullah, Omanii.
I wanna be the kinda father my mother was/
Omanii Abdullah.

p. cm.

ISBN 0-88336-033-0 (pbk.)

1. Afro-American men—Poetry. 2. Readers for new
literates.
I. Title.
PS3551.B3212   1993
811'.54—dc20   92-35328
                                                       CIP

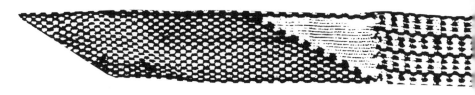

To the Reader

So many negative things have been written about Black males. So little has been done to attack many of the stereotypes about them. In this collection I have tried to remedy this situation in my own way.

The poems in this book include thoughts about Black males, Black pride, relationships, and love. This book includes tributes to James Brown, the Godfather of Soul; Hank Gathers, the Loyola Marymount college basketball player who died from a heart ailment in 1990; and a Black Vietnam veteran.

I try to write about things that have meaning to me, things that have touched my life and made me think, made me react. Sometimes when something happens, and I don't want that feeling to go away, I try to capture it in writing so I can always go back to it.

I hope that when you read the poems, you can feel the joy, the despair, the loneliness, the confusion, and the happiness that's in them.

Listen to these poems as well as read them. When you read the poems to yourself, you can understand them; but when you read the poems aloud, you can feel their meaning.

I speak these poems to myself when I write them. I hope they speak to you.

—Omanii Abdullah

Contents

7   I Wanna Be the Kinda Father
My Mother Was

10   While Sitting in a Harlem Park

11   Ever Notice

12   For You, Hank

13   On the Death of My Grandmother

16   I Never Wanted to Be White

19   Memory Lane

27   Black Vietnam Vet (For William)

30   An Ode of Sorts to James Brown

33   The Guilty—NOT

36   While Waiting for You

37   If I Were You (I'd Fall in Love with Me)

39   When I Think of You

41   Not Even for the Children

42   Pretend

46   Wait a Minute, I Thought You Were Dead

50 Phillip Morris (Not the Cigarette)

52 For Kevin: The Late Speech

54 From Kevin: To My Teacher

56 Do the Right Thing (A Rap Poem)

61 Yeah, You're Right. I'm Not
    Your "Real" Father

I Wanna Be the Kinda Father
My Mother Was

I wanna be the kinda father my mother was
I want that stayin' power
I wanna give you that sense of
"I ain't ever gonna leave you"
Like my mother gave me as my father

I wanna be the one who loves you
        even when you do
What I've told you not to do a hundred times
The one who gets up in the middle
        of the night
To make sure you don't have an accident
        in bed

I remember my mother askin' me
Who did I want to invite
To my birthday party

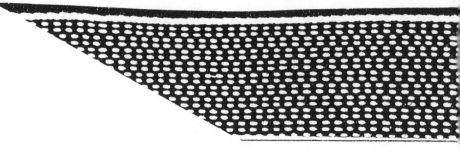

And one day she told some bullies
"Y'all got one more time to run my child home"
And then she looked at me and said
"And you got one more time to let them
Or I'm gonna beat yo ass"

Yeah, I wanna be the kinda father
    my mother was
Who corrected my English when I misspoke
Who showed me through her example
What being a parent is all about
Who laughed at us and made us laugh
Who sat in the bleachers
And cheered my brother on
But couldn't really understand why
He didn't stand for the flag

Harriet Powers (1837–1911), *Pictorial Quilt,* pieced and appliquéd cotton embroidered with yarns, c. 1895–1898. 69 x 105 inches. Bequest of Maxim Karolik. Courtesy, Museum of Fine Arts, Boston.

Who worked overtime at her
    hairdressing profession
To make sure that we were
Some of the best dressed kids
On Easter Sunday
Who loved us through all our ups and downs
And continues to do so
And never, ever seems to grow tired

That's why I wanna be the kinda father
    my mother was
Because if I do it right
Maybe one of my boys will say
"I wanna be the kinda father my dad was"
    And that's the way it's supposed to be!!!

While Sitting in a Harlem Park

While sitting in a Harlem park
I saw a black, furry squirrel
I'd never seen a black squirrel before
And then I saw a pigeon
And as I looked at it
I said, "I'm sure there's
Some beauty there"
But I couldn't see it

While sitting in a Harlem park
I saw this big, fat, yellow woman
Yelling at her son
To go and pee behind
The tree and to shut up
And as I looked at her
I said, "I'm sure there's
Some beauty there"
But I couldn't see it

While sitting in a Harlem park
I saw a man who appeared to be
Down on his luck
He smiled at me
We laughed and talked together
And he told me things
To make me feel good about myself
And I said, "I'm sure there's
Some beauty there"
And I saw it

Ever Notice

Ever notice how it's always quiet
When it snows
Snow descends so unobtrusively
Bringing with it clouds of light
Even on a dismal day
And it makes its entrance so serenely

Ever notice
How unlike rain, which often has
A thunderous introduction
Snow doesn't seem to need
    a round of applause
Before taking the stage

Ever notice

For You, Hank

You went out with a slam dunk
You raced down the court
But the referee blew the whistle
A whistle no one heard but you

The play was over
No more foul shots
No more double fakes
No more rebounds
The referee had called in the "bank man"
You gotta cash in your chips

And even though
I didn't really know you
I miss you, man
Listening to you talk of your aspirations
Made me so proud of you
To know that you had brains
As well as brawn

Well
You made your last slam dunk
I only wish I had known you
Longer and better
'Cause I miss you, man
I miss you, Hank

On the Death of My Grandmother

There were no tears
They had all been cried
They had all been shed
On other occasions

I remember that tin roof house
She called it home
Where when it would rain
Every room had its own private drip

I cried then for her

When we would leave her all alone
In those back woods of Florida
Without indoor plumbing and telephone
And head back to New York
After our summer vacation

I cried then for her

And when her own children started to die
One by one
In the prime of their lives
She was our pillar of strength

I cried then for her

I remember the endless days we shared
Sitting on Aunt Doris' front porch
She telling me stories told before
And my pretending
To hear them for the first time
And feeling just a little sorry for her

I cried then for her

And when I went away to college
I wondered who'd listen to her stories
Who'd appreciate her wry humor
And know that she meant well
And love her like I loved her

And I cried then for her

When I came back home
Her mind had started to falter
And she no longer remembered me
And her conversation was not coherent

And in those last months
When she would just lie in that bed
With the eyes of a frightened child
I would hold her hand
And brush her hair
And talk to her
And her eyes would communicate
What her lips couldn't

And I cried then for her

So when the end finally came
There were no tears
They had all been cried
They had all been shed
On other occasions

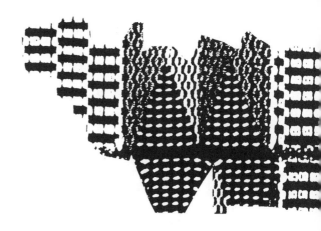

I Never Wanted to Be White

Regardless of how I used to see you
Toss your golden locks
And flick your hair out of the way
    of your baby blue eyes
And see your movie stars
Run their fingers through it
And wonder how it must feel
To have your fingers glide through
That silky silkiness
Even with all that
I never wanted to be white

And as a youngster when I watched TV
I seldom saw me
But I saw you bigger than life
With your six-shooters, super powers,
    bosomy blondes
And they did appear to have more fun
I must admit

Yet

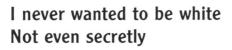

I never wanted to be white
Not even secretly

And when I saw
How much political power you wielded
How you controlled the lives of so many
How you always seemed to be able
To manipulate to your advantage
And make the other guy
Look like the one in the wrong

Still

I never wanted to be white

Because I always had a sense of who I was
Long before brother Jackson
Told us we were somebody

And I know amidst the lies
Told to me about me
By you
That we were and always have been
A mighty race
Prone to emerge victorious against our foes

So

I never wanted to be white
Because I felt no shame
In my kinky hair and thick lips
Your slander didn't bother me
Your oppression, if anything
Made me stronger
And forced me (and I thank you)
Deeper into myself
Loving me

Which is why
I never
Ever
Wanted to be white

David MacDonald, *Covered Jar # 4*,
stoneware, 1971. 28 inches.
Private collection.

Memory Lane

We're going to take a little trip
Of days gone by
Of Butterfly McQueen
And a dance called the popeye

When drugs were a thing
Reserved for people of the stage
And even among them
Only a rare few would engage

A little trip down
What I call Memory Lane
Remember Sam Cooke
Working on that "Chain Gang"

And watching the TV
But never seeing us
Then in '56 Rosa Parks said
"Hell if I'm gonna sit in the back
of the bus"

Not today, my friend
She said she was rather beat
And it was at that point
That the then "Negro" hit the street

And after years of struggling
Some changes were made
Because our forefathers knew
Some dues had to be paid

Remember Chubby Checker
As he did the twist
And the African queen Nina
With those luscious thick lips

Did you have "block" parties
That cost a quarter to get in
You stayed until twelve
When your mom told you to be back
    by ten

And your little grade school
With not one Black male teacher
But the neighborhood was jumpin'
With bootleg Sunday preachers

Now who could forget the Motown Revue
You couldn't wait till it came to town
Asking your girl if she wanted to go
And her saying, "You know I'm down"

The Temptations had moves
That were, well, outta sight
After one of their shows
You'd go home and practice them all night

"Please Mr. Postman"
And the "Duke of Earl"
Those bad Supremes
Now they were my girls

Always afraid when you cut class
That you knew somebody would tell
And you knew if your folks knew
You would certainly catch hell

The food even seemed better
Mom frying up that chicken
And if she caught you stealing a piece
You might just get a lickin'

Could leave your toys outside
And they'd be there the next day
Try that now
Huh—no way, José

Kids had more respect
For older people and such
Nowadays parents tell you up front
"My child don't you dare touch"

As a child you had no worries
Just how to have fun
Now don't be surprised
If you hear a twelve-year-old saying
  "That's my son"

The heroes we have
Are so very few
Some of the things you see them doing
You want to ask is that what's important
  to you

Look at Ali and O.J.
And football great Jim Brown
Seems I'm always reading about him
Throwing some woman down

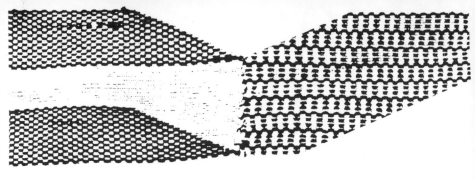

But we do have Martin and Malcolm
Who tried to stand tall
And many others who were
Constantly backed up against the wall

And to make us laugh
We had "Moms" and Redd Foxx
Dancers like Sammy Davis
Who was far from orthodox

There was the social unrest
Of 1965
Which the press called riots
But we know the press is jive

We shed the label of "colored"
And eventually "Negro" too
Now we "Black" people do some things
That an imbecile wouldn't do

We went through the age
Of the "process" head
And now with the Gerri curl
Our head is still dead

Little Stevie Wonder
Writes songs for you to ponder
His magical lyrics
Seldom allow your mind to wander

Lest I forget Smokey
Marvin, Billie, and the "DUKE"
The book and the movie
About the invisible spook

You know the one
That sat by the door
And Richard Wright's Bigger Thomas
Who wanted only a little more

A little more out of life
Was that asking too much?
Or as we're always being told
You gotta take it slow—don't rush

Four dead Sunday school girls
And a Mississippi leader
Who left a young daughter
That her mother wonders who will feed her

And I guess I could go on and on
Recounting the joy and the pain
Yet I hope you've enjoyed
This brief trip down Memory Lane

Black Vietnam Vet (For William)

They tell me
U usta be so vibrant
U made people laugh
Now U make people cry
'Cause they feel sorry for U
'Cause they see what war did to U
And your country closes
A blind eye to U

U usta be
A sometime would-be musician
Playing a little jive-time jazz
Nothin' serious
But U don't remember none of that
And now U play the blues
Big time

My country 'tis of thee
O say can you see
What you've done to my brother
In the name of liberty

U usta be
One hell of an artist
They tell me U could draw
Anything, man
And the conclusion
That I now draw is that
Your mind is void of
Any remembrance of such

The only thing U draw now
Is your hand from the bottle
To your lips
And I want to help U
But U won't let me touch U

U usta be
Somebody's husband and father
Somebody's son and brother
But now U feel U are nobody
All alone
The war killed U

Aaron Douglas, *Into Bondage,* oil on canvas, 1936. 60 x 60 inches.
Evans-Tibbs Collection, Washington, D.C.

And U feel it's only a matter of time
Before U die
I'd like to do something for U
We have so much in common
We share so much
But U won't let me touch U

Why?
I am not your enemy
I want to be your friend
Your brother
But U won't let me touch U
U just won't let me touch U

An Ode of Sorts to James Brown

Uh
Good God
James Brown's in jail
Ain't got nobody to pay his bail

And now what did
Mr. Please Please Please do?

He was no mastermind of Watergate
Those criminals doin' time
In country club jails
Where they contemplate
About the millions of dollars
From books they'll earn
When much too soon to society
They'll return

James Brown's in jail
Ain't got nobody to go his bail

I feel like I wanna break out
Dunt, dunt, dunt, dunt
In a coooold sweat
Dunt, dunt, dunt, dunt
Hit me

Just what did
The hardest working man
In show business do?

He didn't sleep with Marilyn Monroe
Like somebody else did
Y'all used to love so
He didn't sell no arms to Iran
Just told Black people to take a stand

Told us once to say it loud
That we are Black, that we are proud
And now James Brown's in jail
And for him have we failed

'Cause there was a time
When he used to dance
There was a time when he used to prance
But you can bet
You haven't seen nothing yet
Until you see him do the James Brown
Aw

Good God
My man . . . James Brown
Doin' time
Ain't it a drag
That papa's got a brand new bag?
Dun, dun, dun, dun, dun, dun, dun

But he's probably still grinning
'Cause he's living in America
But he's in jail
Living in America
Can't pay his bail
Living in America
Living in America
Live
Vin
In
America

And I can't stand it
Good God

The Guilty—NOT

I think what did it was the word "baton"
You know
What a cheerleader uses
She twirls it
She tosses it
She says "rah, rah, rah"
But the cops who used it on Rodney
Didn't twirl it
Didn't toss it
They just beat the hell out of him
Cheering
"Get up, son-of-a-bitch"
Wap
"Get up, asshole"
Wap, wap
"Get up, niggah"
Wap, wap, wap
With a "baton"

We used to call it a nightstick
Yeah, a billy club
But never a "baton"
Because we knew it wasn't a playthang
And we knew when we saw it
In the hands of the Man
He meant business
And we knew if he used it
It was for real
And now the "baton twirlers"
Have been found guilty—NOT
And it's another sad indictment
On our society

I suppose it was
A jury of "their" peers
But where's the jury of Rodney's peers?

And are we gonna sit
On the sideline
As injustice passes us by?
Because this was a blow
Not only to Rodney
BUT TO ALL BLACK MEN
Wap
What we gonna do?
Wap, wap
Spike keeps telling us we gotta wake up
Wap, wap, wap
Because the guilty have been found
NOT GUILTY
NOT GUILTY
NOT GUILTY

NOT GUILTY!

Charles Searles, *Filàs for Sale*
(from *Nigerian Impressions*
series), acrylic on canvas, 1972.
72 x 52 inches. Courtesy of the
Museum of the National Center
of Afro-American Artists, Inc.,
Boston.

While Waiting for You

I set a place for you
At the dinner table
And look across
Knowing that one day soon
Your face I'll see
Your voice I'll hear
Your smile will illuminate the room
These are thoughts I have
While waiting for you

I go to the park
And see people who appear to be
So much in love
Strolling hand in hand
Their eyes communicating
Feelings of warmth and trust
And I sit alone
While waiting for you

I lie alone at night
Listening to romantic songs
Longing to look over and see you
And hold you
And wake up next to you
And one day soon I will
These are thoughts I have
While waiting for you

If I Were You (I'd Fall in Love with Me)

If you've had trouble with love
And about to give up
There's something
That I'd like to say
If you're in need of someone
Who's tender and kind
All you need is to look my way

For I too have been hurt
And know how it feels
And can empathize
With the pain in your heart
If you desire someone
To treat you tenderly
Then if I were you
I'd fall in love with me

I don't mean to boast
Or brag on myself
But I do believe in
Speaking the truth
I don't have time
For silly mind games
Please don't be fooled by my youth

To me love is a serious venture
One that should be full
Of sweet harmony
And if it is that
That you are longing for
Then if I were you
I'd fall in love with me

I won't promise you
The sun, moon, or stars
For I'd only be telling a lie
But something I know I can give
Is something that money can't buy

I'll always be me, just myself
I'll put on no airs for others to see
So if you think
You want to take a chance
Then if I were you
I'd fall in love with me

When I Think of You

It may sound strange
But sometimes I miss you
Even when we're together
Because I don't seem to appreciate you
Until we are apart

I let the diversions of our day-to-day existence
Interfere with my being myself
And letting you know how very much
You mean to me

And when I let moments slip away
Without sharing with you my thoughts of love
I hurt afterwards

Yet I continue to wound myself
By torturing my being
By not being honest

And the truth of the matter is
That you make me feel so special
With simple things
Like
How do I look?
Do you like this dress?
What do you think I should do?
It matters to me
That I matter that much to you

And when I think of you
Your patience
Your smile
Your gratitude
It makes all the hard times
The struggles
The hanging in there
All worthwhile

That is
When I think of you

Not Even for the Children

I tried though
And the years kept mounting up
The resentment getting stronger
And the love . . .
Whatever love there had been
Had ebbed away

The touch and kisses had become distant
As I tried to distance myself from you
Sex, not lovemaking, had become perfunctory
And I loathed what I once loved

Yet I kept struggling
Kept hanging in there
Lying in bed praying I could fall asleep
Before you accidentally
Touched, rubbed, moved up against me
Avoiding eye contact
For fear my eyes would say
What my lips wouldn't
Couldn't
Muster up the courage to

And then one bright sunshiny morning
My heart could keep quiet no more
With tears pouring from my insides
I quit the charade and faced the hard fact
That I could no longer live like this
Not even for the children

Lois Mailou Jones,
The Ascent of Ethiopia,
oil on canvas, 1932.
23½ x 17¼ inches.
Collection of the artist.

Pretend

When you're alone you do crazy things
When nobody's looking you pretend
At least I know I do

And if you say you don't
Well
Then
You're doing it right now

Sometimes I pretend that
I'm receiving a Grammy
For one of my poems
And in my acceptance speech
I thank ALLAH, my parents, my lovely wife
My friends Dawud and Shahid
Who always read my poems
My brother Ted for encouraging me
And my fifth-grade teacher, Mrs. Colbert

Of course I know
You don't get Grammies for poems
But hey, this is my pretend

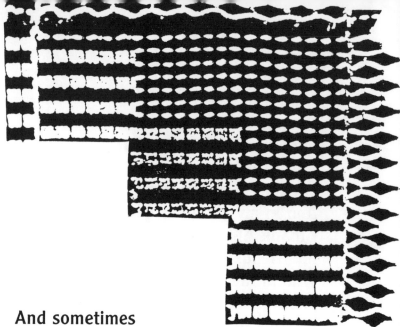

And sometimes
I pretend that I'm Michael, Magic,
    and Dr. J
All rolled into one
And I be
Yeah, I be slam dunkin' for days
Remaining ever so humble
And modest of course

And then sometimes I pretend
That my children think
I'm the greatest dad in the world
And when called upon and asked
Who was instrumental in their lives
I hope they'll say
Next to GOD of course
Yeah, it was you, Dad

And then sometimes
When I'm driving all alone
I pretend that
I'm the love crooner Luther
And believe me
I could turn your house into a home
(Sung à la Luther Vandross)
'Cause you're not meant to live alone

And when I climb the stairs
And turn my key
All I want to know is one thing
Are you gonna be, say you gonna be
Are you gonna beeeeee
Well, welllll
Still in love
Still in love, still in love
Stillllll in lovvvvvvve
Witttttttt Meeeeeeeeee

And that I hope will be
No PRETEND

Wait a Minute, I Thought You Were Dead

Do you remember Art Linkletter
He had a TV program a few years ago
When he talked with little children
Right near the end of the show
And as he said
Children say the darndest things

Well, I can remember
When my friend's dad
Who had been married twice
Lost wife #2
Who incidentally
Was not made of sugar and spice

And his son, my friend, told his kids
That his father's wife had died
Not making it clear to them
That it was wife #2
And not wife #1, his mother
Who had been the first bride

So lo and behold the next week
When he ventured to visit his mom
She said, "Ted
Your youngest daughter just looked at me
Her grandmother
And quipped, 'What are you doing here?
Wait a minute
I thought you were dead!'"

My friend looked funny and strange
As the little girl said
"I thought you said
Grandma was dead"
And the real grandma
Raised up from her chair
As she didn't like wife #2
Being called Grandma in her stead

You see there was no love lost
Between the two
And so my friend is trying to think
What to say
As his precocious little daughter
Surveys her grandma
Saying, "For you to be dead
You sure look OK"

His mother is now fuming
And with her heart condition
She may soon join wife #2
So my friend says to his child
"Go out and play"
But his mother said, "No, honey, baby
What else did your dad have to say?"

"Well, he said that Grandma was sick
But I see you lying in bed
And my father never tells me lies
Wait a minute
You sure you're not dead?

"'Cause my father said
The angels came to get you
As you were sick and couldn't get well
And that you had gone to heaven"
To which the mother said
"That ole winch has gone to hell"

And grandma #1 told the child
"I'm your only grandma
And on that subject enough said"
But the little girl still looking puzzled
Said, "Daddy, I guess she ain't dead!"

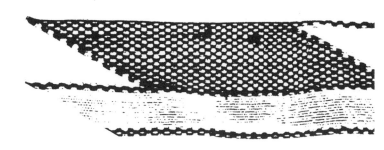

Phillip Morris (Not the Cigarette)

I used to see you
Going to and fro to work
In your white shirt and tie
Polished shoes and briefcase

And I was so proud of you
Little brother
For in you I could see the promise
Of a better and brighter tomorrow

And then
I met an old acquaintance of yours
And he said

"I know this Phillip Morris
You're always talking about;
We get drunk together"

Ed Love, *Mask for Mingus,* welded steel,
1974. 51 x 34 x 9 inches. Collection of
the artist.

And I retorted
Defensively
Protecting the honor and good name
Of my little brother
"You must be mistaken
You don't get drunk with Phillip Morris"

And when I saw you I asked you
And you embarrassingly said
"I
I
I
I used to, I mean, a long time ago
But I don't no more"

And I was glad to hear that
Because when I look at you
I look at you with the eyes
Of a father to his son
And I see the promise of so much in you

And hey
I love you, little brother

For Kevin: The Late Speech

The assignment was to give a speech
On someone you admired

The speech was late
I told him he'd get a letter grade cut
He said he didn't mind

He opened his mouth and spoke
Like I'd never heard him speak before
I was mesmerized
By the words he put together
To extol the virtues
Of his dad
And I secretly envied his father
For having a son like him

The speech was late
But there would be no letter grade cut
How could I?

I wrote on his critique sheet
"Be sure and let your dad know
How you feel about him"

But he was absent the following few days
And I couldn't give him his paper
With my words of advice

And when he returned
He apologized for his absence
I gave him his paper feeling proud of myself
For the advice I'd written at the bottom
He turned to me and said
"Mr. Abdullah
. . . My father died over the weekend
But I had already told him
What you just now suggested"

At that moment I felt a closeness to him
And we embraced
Student and professor
Black and white
One with a father and one fatherless
And he said he sensed I understood
And I sensed I did

So, you see
The speech wasn't late
After all!

From Kevin: To My Teacher

*The previous poem was written about my student Kevin
Madden. When he read it, he wrote this poem in response.*

The words jumped out and strangled
my emotions.
"Make sure to tell your father that
you love him,
I'm sure he would like to know."
For on his deathbed I took
the advice I was to get days later.

Like a plague,
I could not prepare for the death
of my father.
But the Lord sent me a
ray of hope.
He was my speech teacher,
a Muslim of stern patience
and virtue.

His guidance and advice to me in
such dire straits
blanketed my shiver of sorrows.
His friendly embrace held together
my love for my father and
kept me safe from destruction.

My father always said, "with death
comes joy,"
and my teacher was mine.

I don't see my teacher
much anymore,
but he is always on my mind.
Never have I been touched so
deeply by another man.
His love and caring is endless,
and I hope one day,
to be half the man
that he is now.

Do the Right Thing (A Rap Poem)

For the longest time I hated rap
I thought it was just a bunch of crap
To me they all sounded the same
Same rhyme, same beat
But yo another name to the game
Check it out

I guess 'cause I'm a parent
And I ain't hip
My boys say you on a mission, Dad
A serious trip
Yeah, it's a trip all right
One that's full of hope
Where you can succeed
But you say it ain't too dope

It ain't too cool to be smart in class
So you gotta be the clown
And show your ass
But I'm fast on the court
When I play b-ball
You don't go to study hall
And I know you drink alcohol

I bought my boy a watch
That he says he can't wear
As his posse might think
He was rather square
But it's dope to wear your clothes
Inside out
And get weird haircuts
Know what I'm talkin' about?

James Phillips, *Mojo,*
acrylic on canvas (jute),
1987. 114 x 66 inches.
Courtesy, Dallas Museum
of Art.

Sometimes I wonder
Did I do this to my dad?
I say, "Good God
Could I have been this mad?"
You know you always runnin'
A weak-whack game
But the lines and the moves
Are all the same

The lies you tell now
I've heard before
Some of them I tried
That's why I know the score
Yo Dad, remember the line
The Fresh Prince ran?
I guess he was right
"Parents just don't understand"

And this is a song that I hate to sing
But all I want from you is to
"Do the right thing"
Yeah
"Do the right thing"
Yo man
"Do the right thing"
Do you know, do you know, do you know,
   do you know

Now I'm not tryin' to keep you
From havin' fun
But there's a job
That has to be done
Life for Blacks ain't no big party
Dam
The Man ain't waiting for you to say
"Yo, here I am"

I know, Dad
We gotta work hard to be our best
As there will always be
Some kind of test
And as the days go by
You get older 'n older
And I won't always be
Lookin' over your shoulder

2 4 6 8 and 10
Be careful who you choose
As your friend
Your partner may be smilin'
All in your face
All the time plottin'
To take your place

I want you to learn how
To think with your head
And not the stick
Between your legs
Spreadin' your seed all over the land
Makin' a baby
Doesn't prove you're a man

Bein' a man means
Takin' care of the child
And we don't mean just
Every once in a while
Nintendo and Sega are games you play
But babies are real
And need their daddies every day

You see people dealin' drugs in the streets
Dressin' fine, turnin' tricks
For their treats
Tellin' you that they know
What's up
They don't really
'Cause drugs is kickin' their butts
And all we want from you is to
"Do the right thing"

Yeah, You're Right. I'm Not Your "Real" Father

Mama said there'd be days like this
There'd be days like this Mama said

You know it bothers me when I watch TV
And I always see these athletes waving
And saying "hi" to their moms
Not that I have anything against mothers
Mind you
But I just wonder
Don't none of y'all have daddies
You wanna say "hi" to?

Anderson Pigatt, *Caught in the Middle Earth,* wood and paint, 1970. 28 x 11 x 19 inches. Photo: DMA Photography. Schomburg Center for Research in Black Culture, Art & Artifacts Division, The New York Public Library, Astor, Lenox, and Tilden Foundations.

So the next time
You wanna jump in my face with
"Yo man, you ain't my real daddy"
Yeah, you're right
I'm not your "real" father

I'm just the man who gets up
    out of his bed
To put extra blankets on you
When I think your room is too cold

I'm the one that stands out in the rain
To watch you while you play
Little league football

I'm the one who held you
And tried to comfort you
When you sprained
Your wrist and thought you were dying

I'm the one who feels bad
'Cause all your teammates have
    $100 Nikes on
But I can't afford to buy you a pair
But yeah, you're right
I'm not your "real" father

I'm just the one
Who picks you up from work
So you don't have to
Stand out in the rain
Waiting for a bus

I'm the one
That your principal has gotten to know
On a first-name basis
Because he sees me so often
And it's not because your ass is so good
Either

I'm the one who took a part-time job
So that I could afford to buy you
And your brother a bicycle

I'm the one who compliments you
On jobs well done

I'm the one who's trying to give you
A sense of direction
So that maybe one day
When you grow up
And if you should have an athletic son
That ever has a need
To look into a TV camera
He just might want to say
"Hi Dad"

So yeah, you're right
I'm not your "real" father
I'm just the man who loves you!